I DON'T KNOW WHAT I'M COLORING! BOOK
VOLUME 2!

The book which reveals itself to you.

Just begin coloring INSIDE the lines, as they grow thicker and thi...

FEELING SURPRISED IS NICE, RIGHT?

Are you ready to color WITHOUT KNOWING WTF you're coloring?

This is that kind of book.

You need to be a little different for this one.

A little more badass.

Start coloring inside the spiral and let yourself discover.

You will discover so many things about yourself in the time you just fill and fill and fill the spirals...

*ALL THE IMAGES ARE REVEALED ON THE LAST PAGE. BUT DON'T PEEK.

Start with black or start with colored pencils.

That's the only decision you need to make.

Then, just start filling the lines and follow the spiral...

AND OFF INTO THE JOURNEY WE GO...

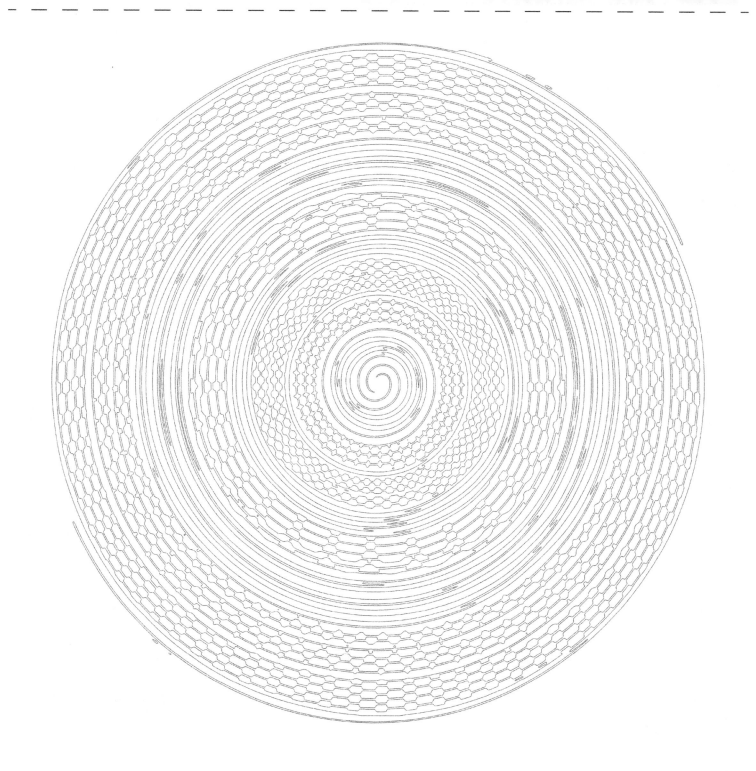

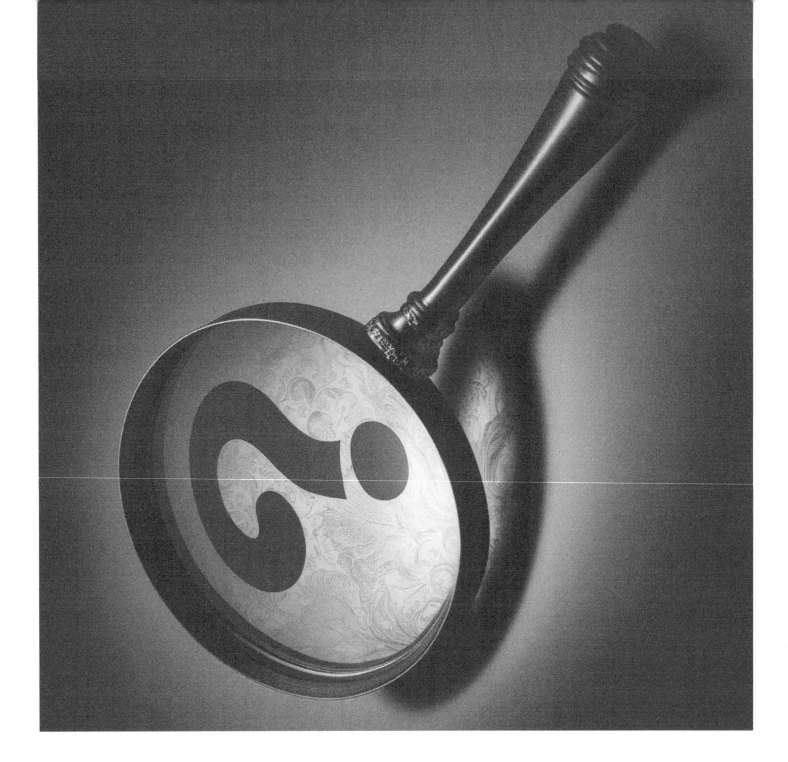

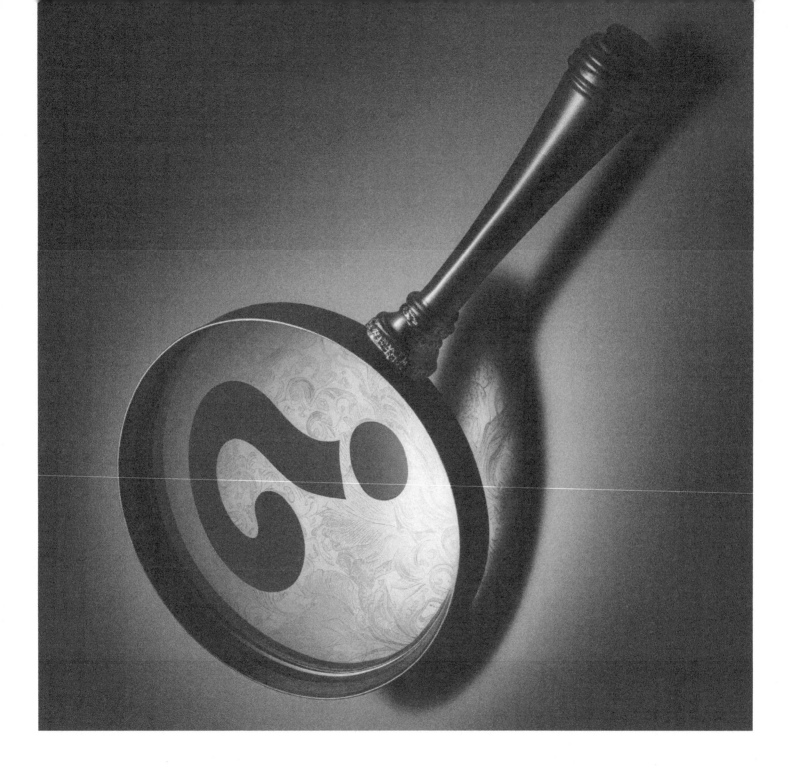

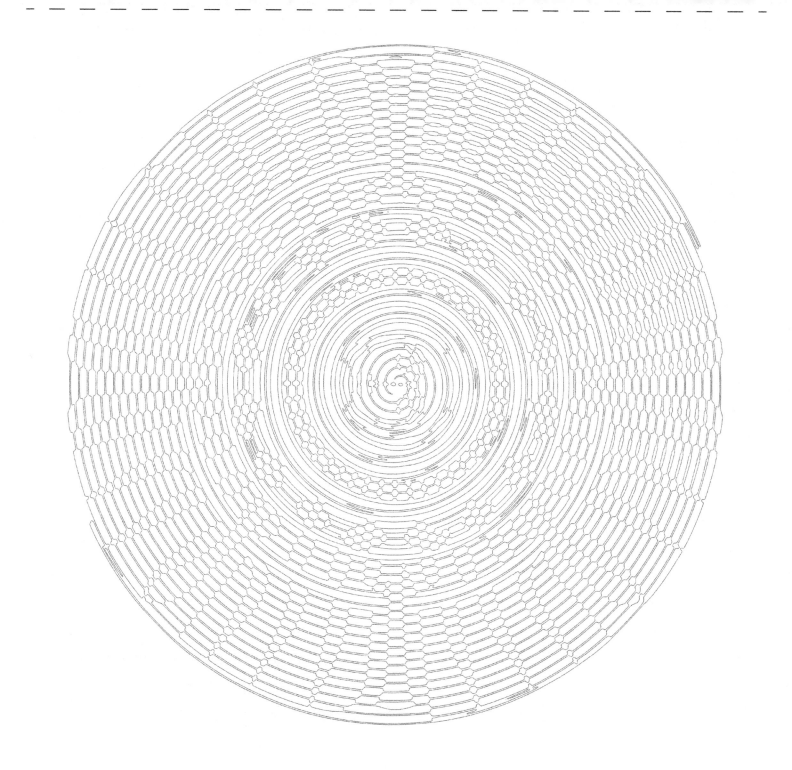

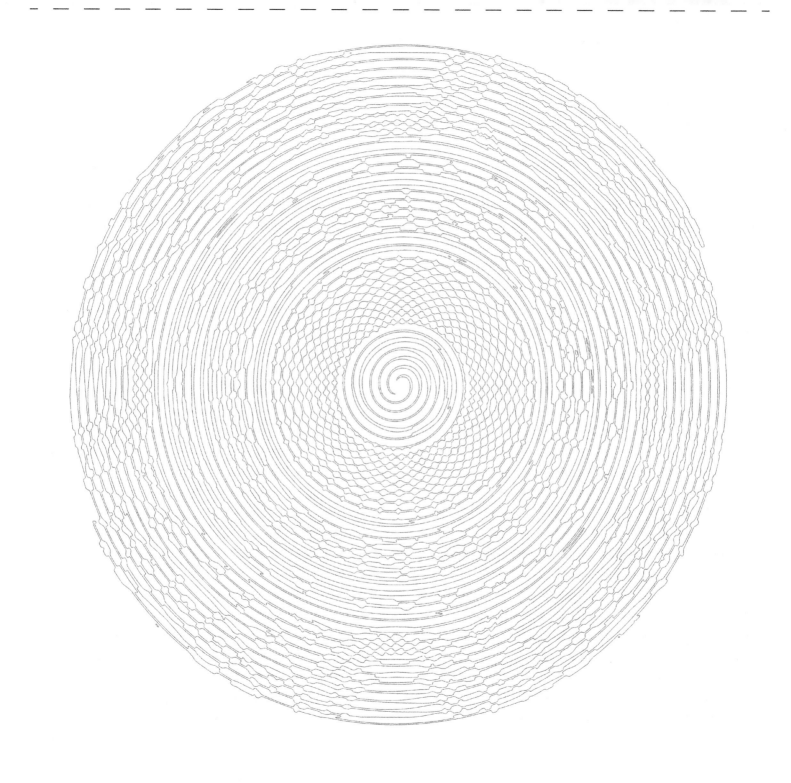

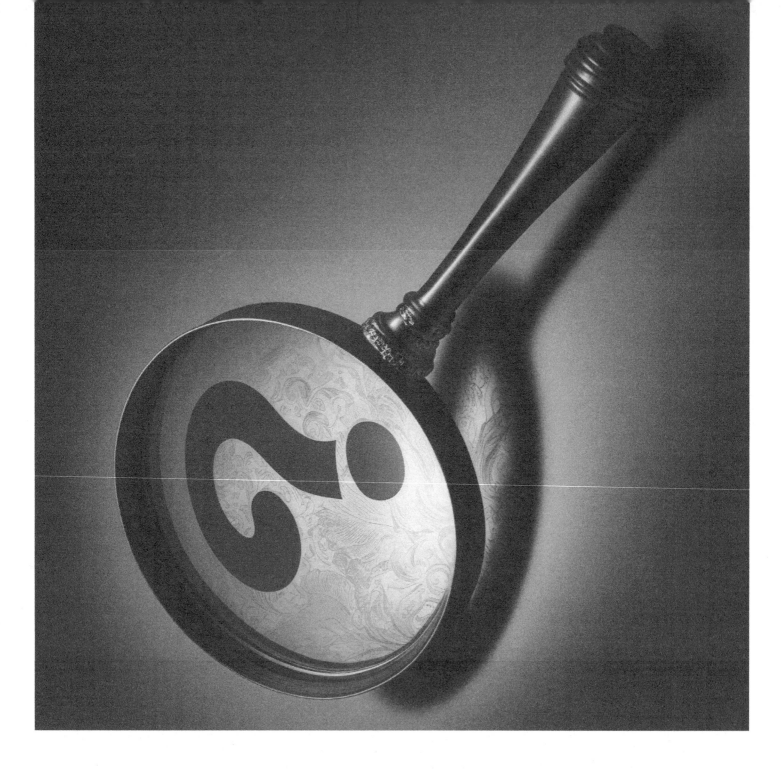

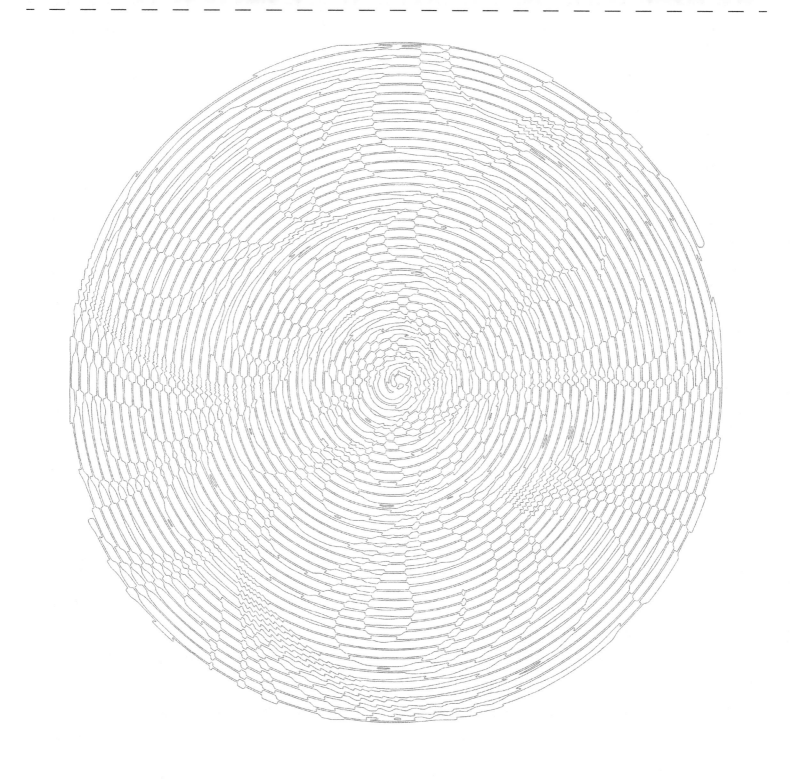

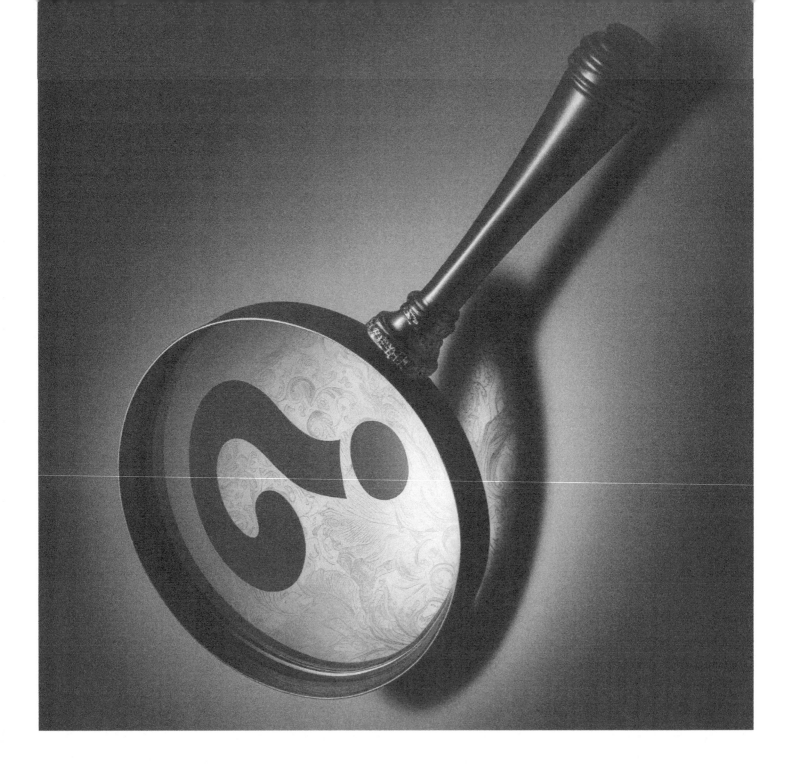

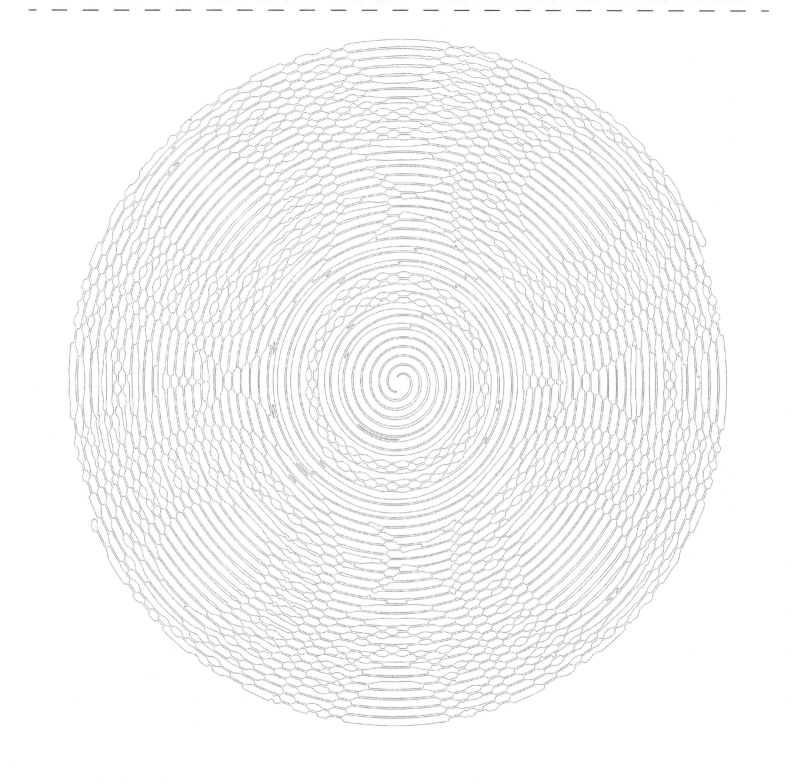

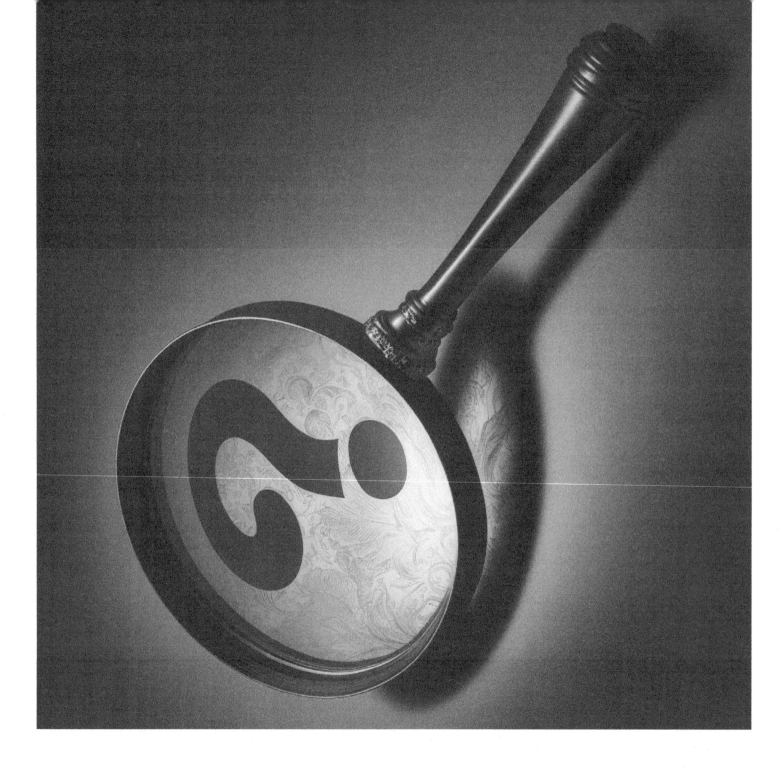

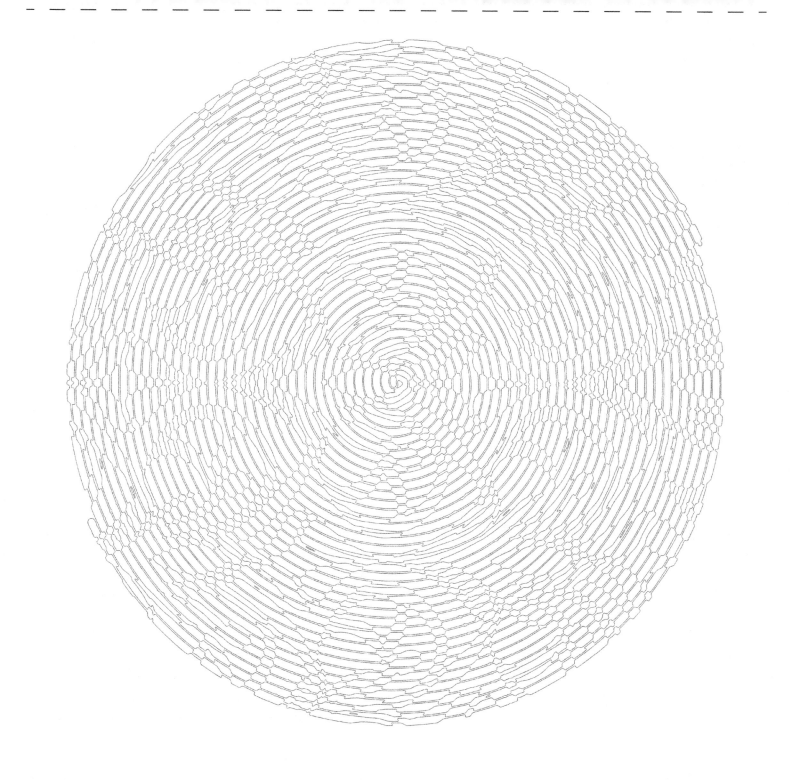

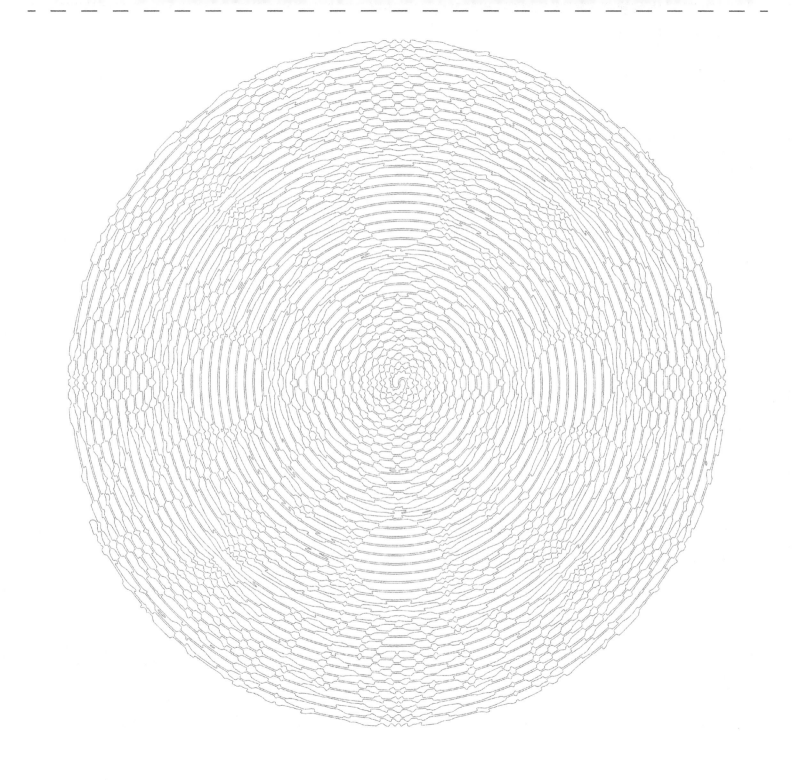

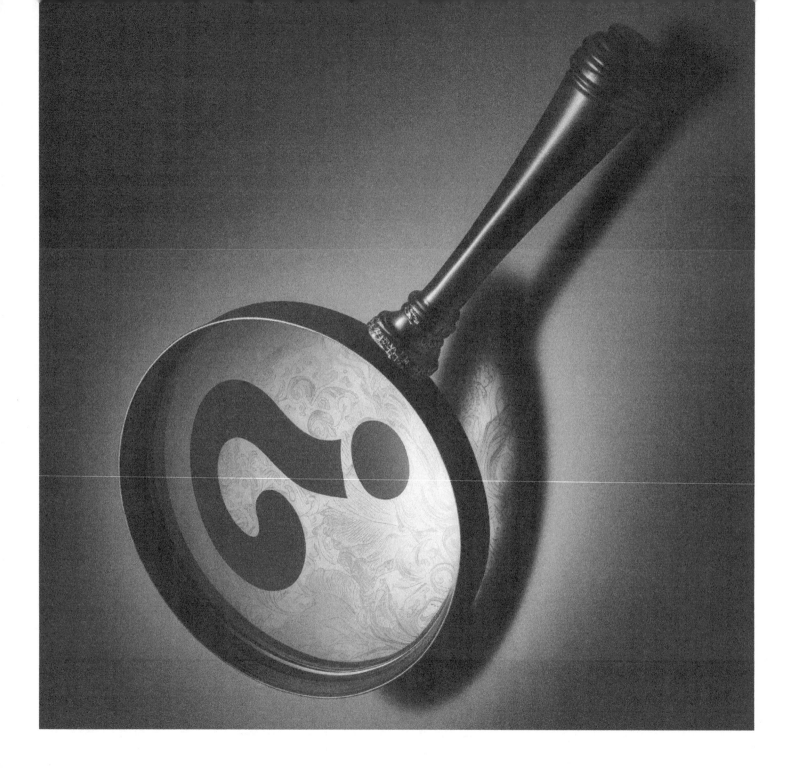

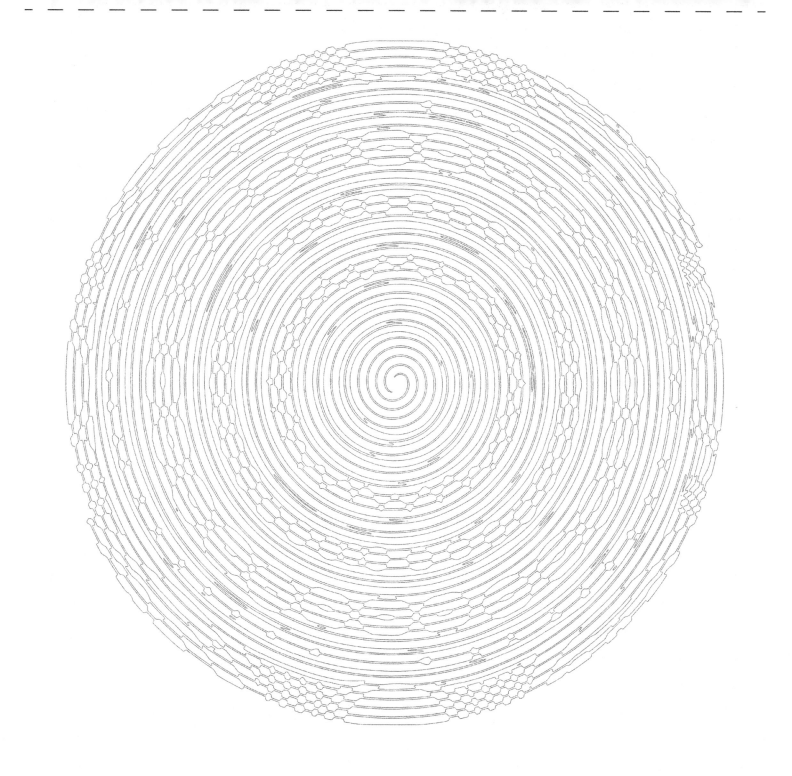

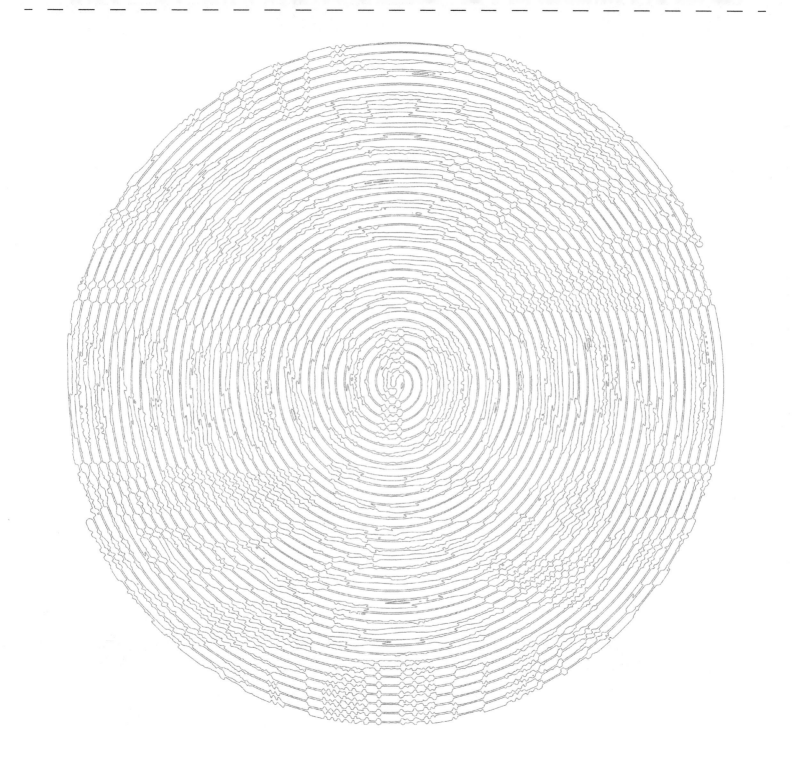

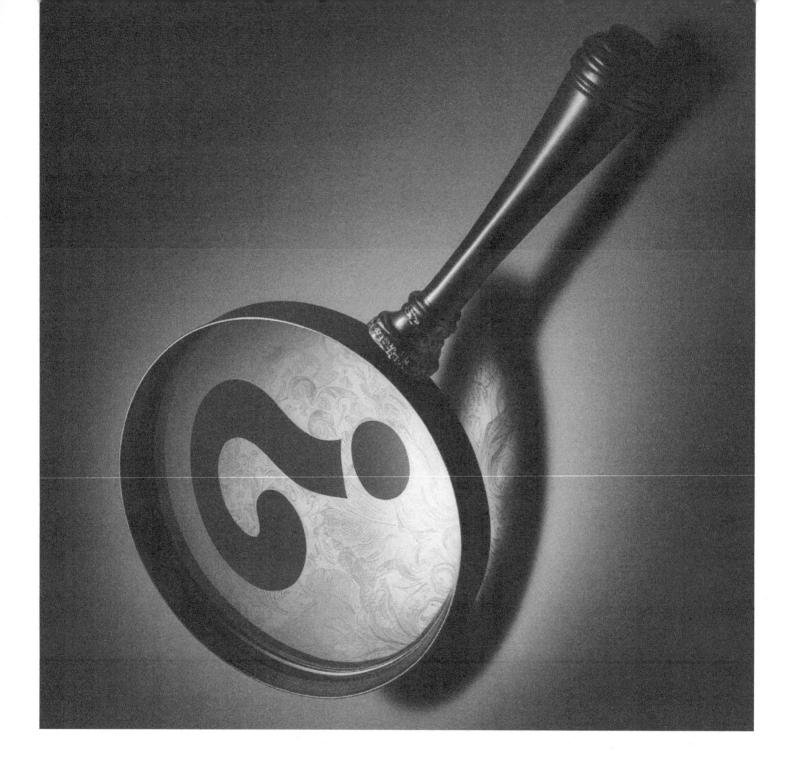

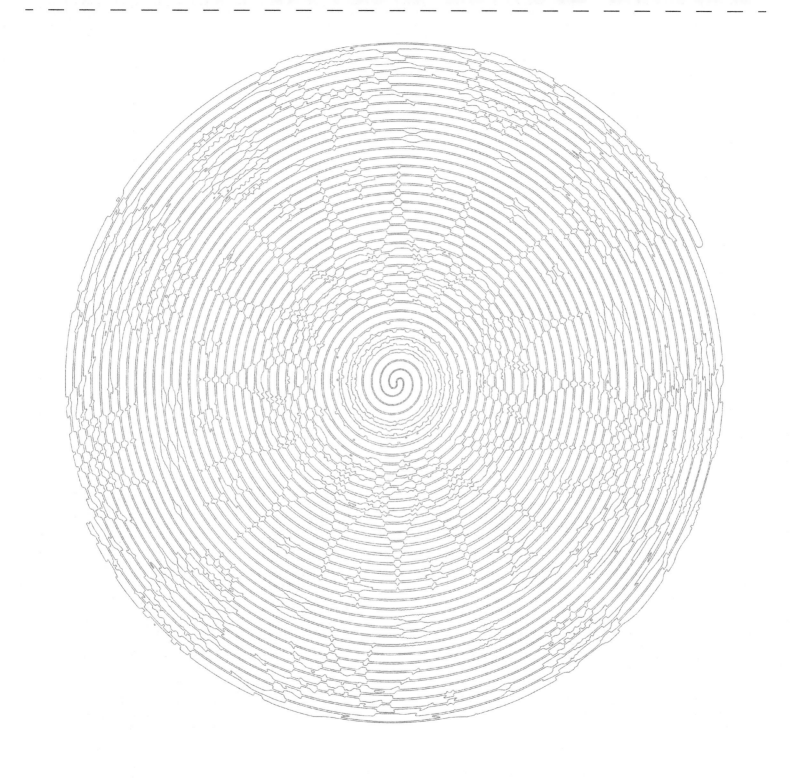

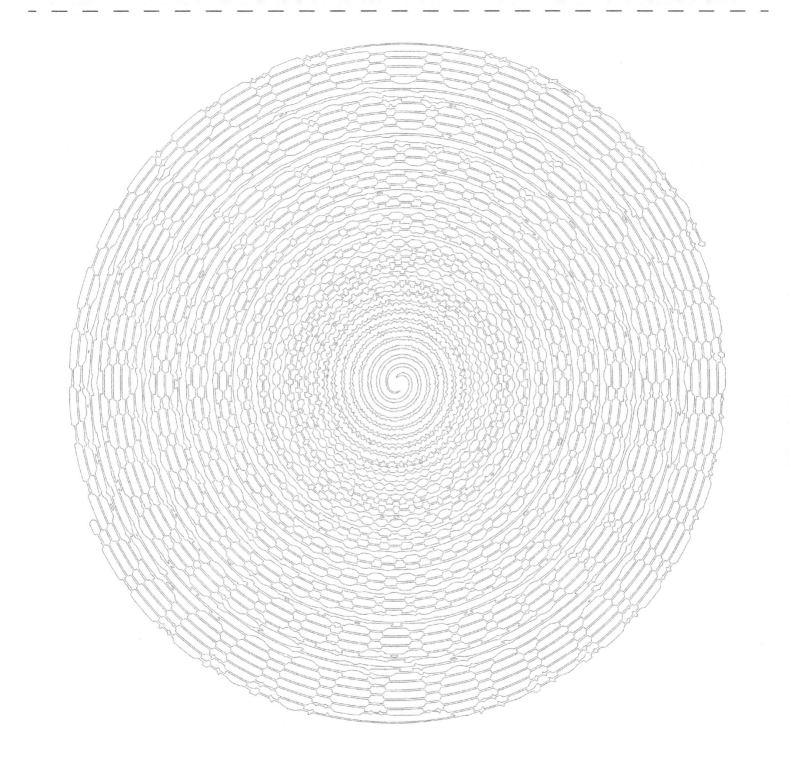

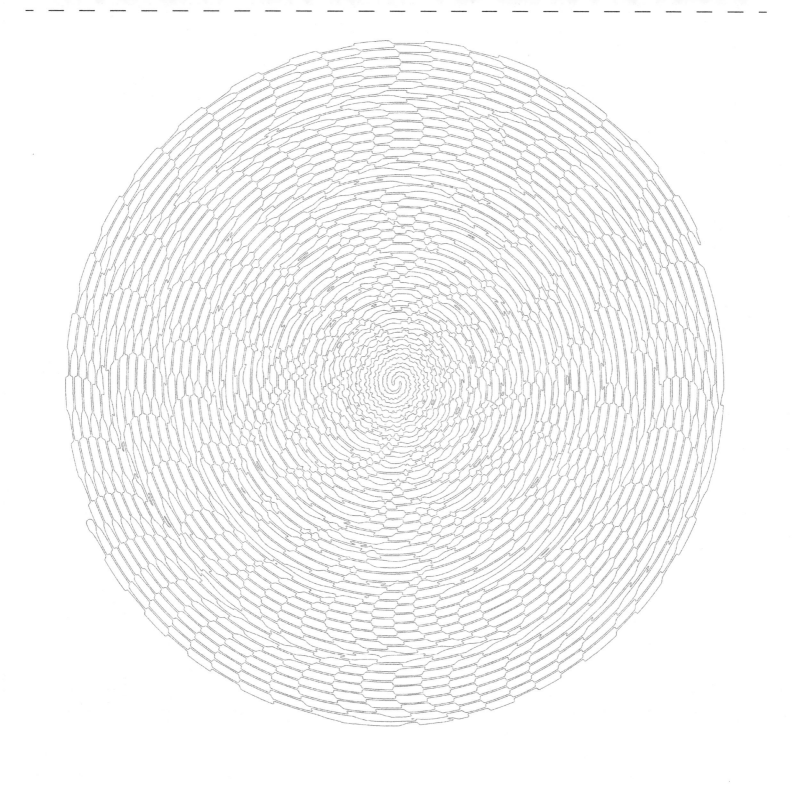

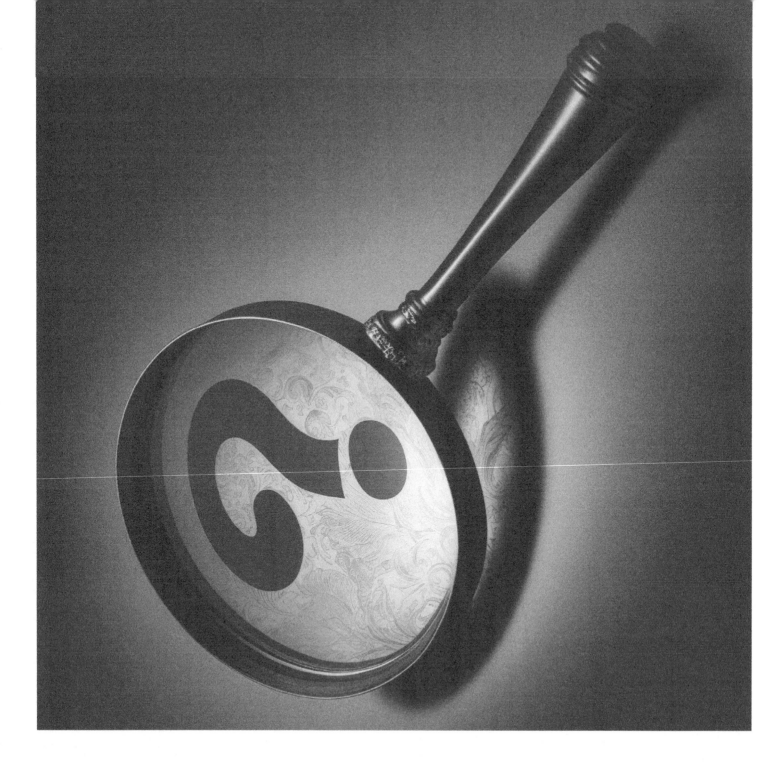

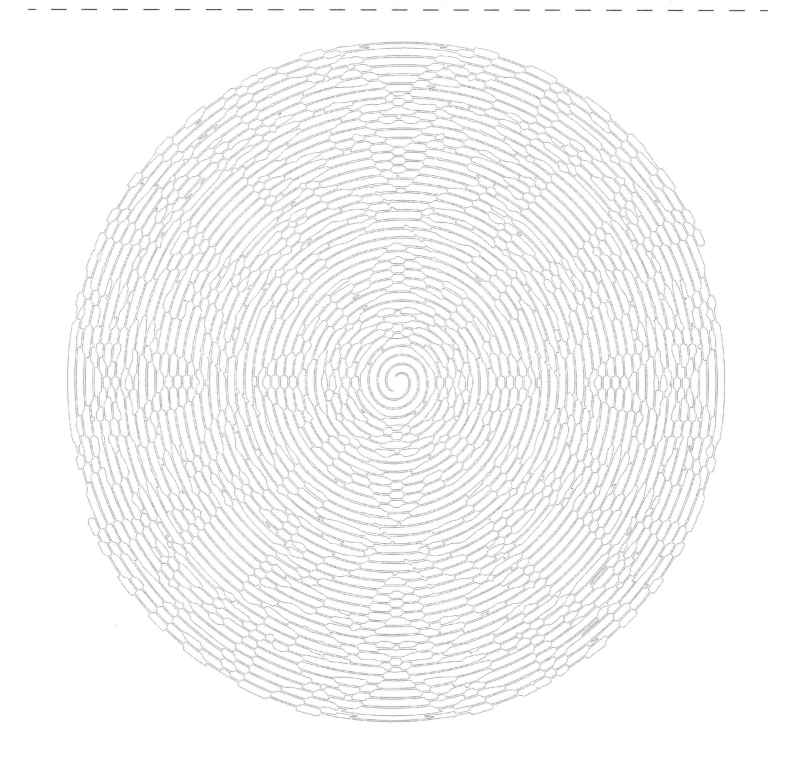

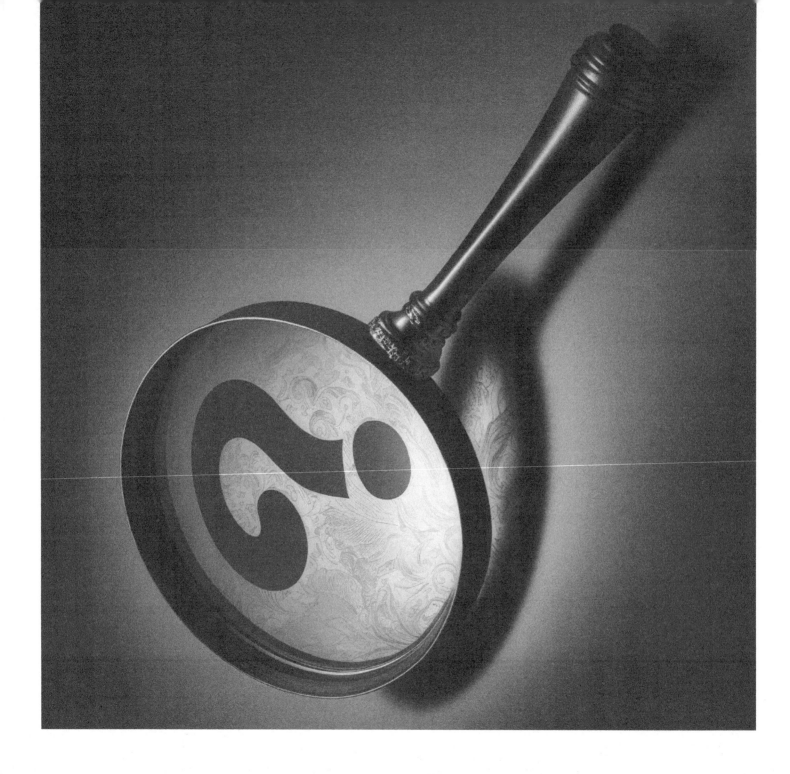

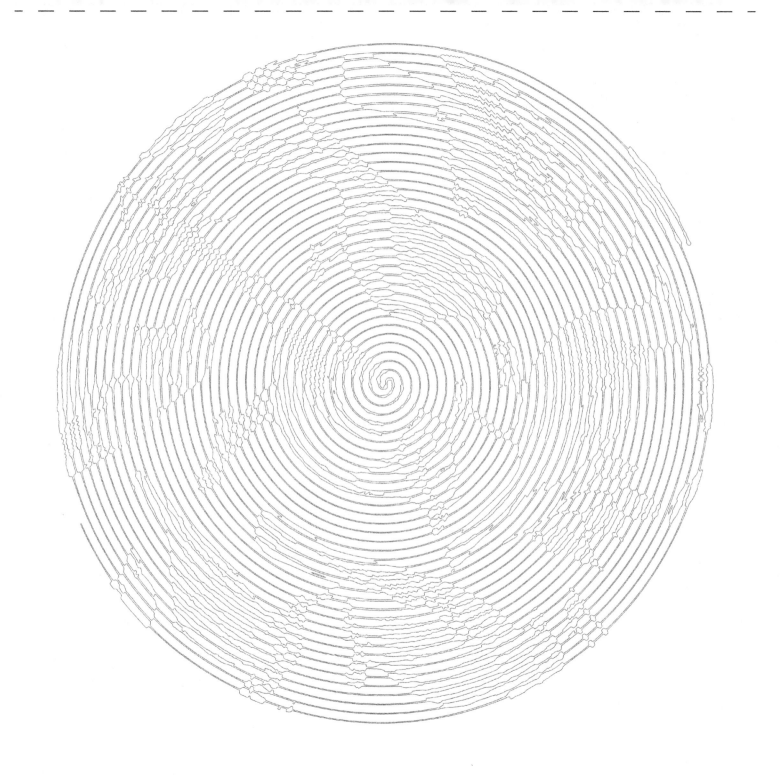

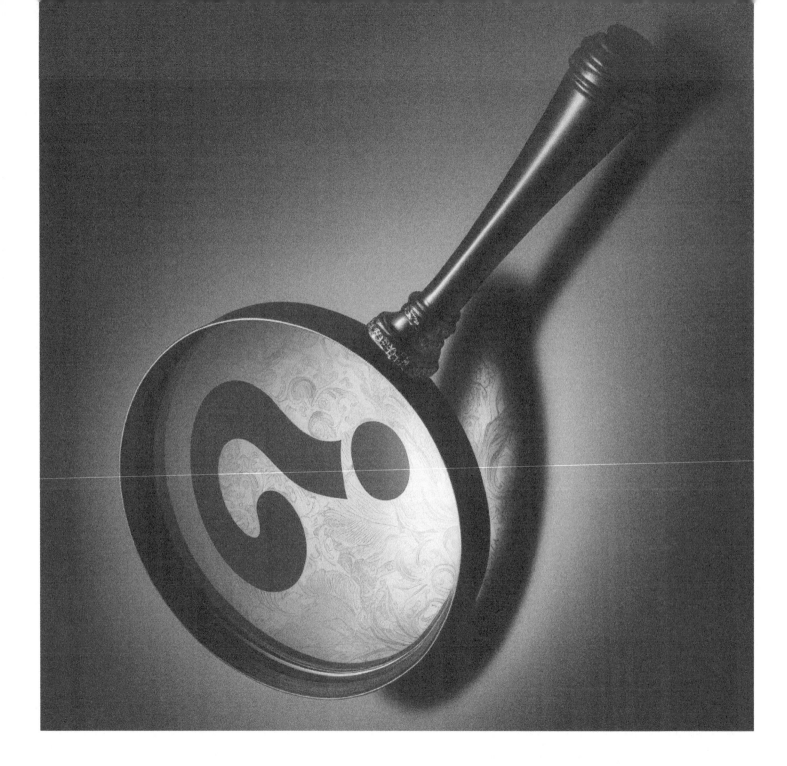

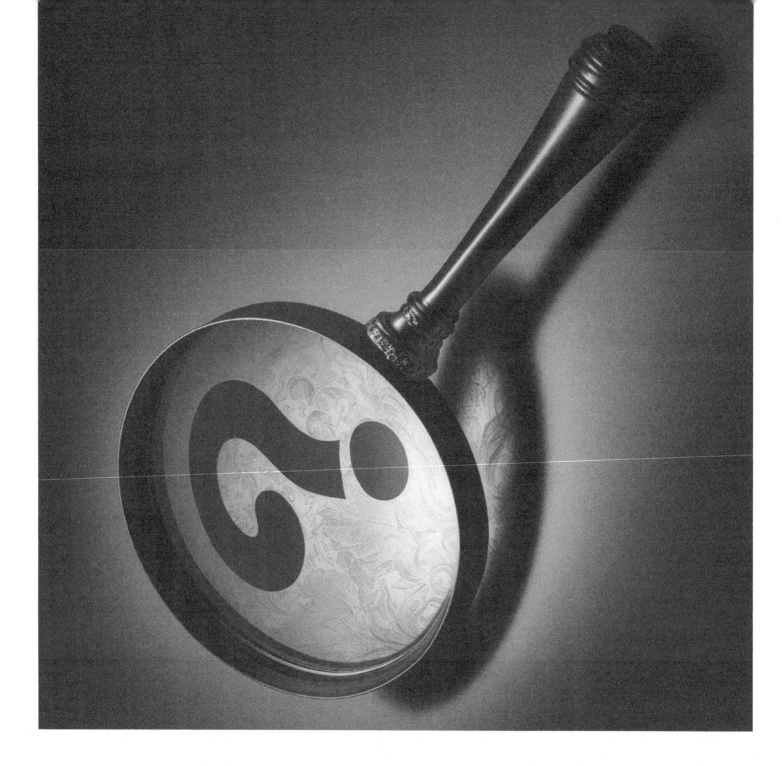

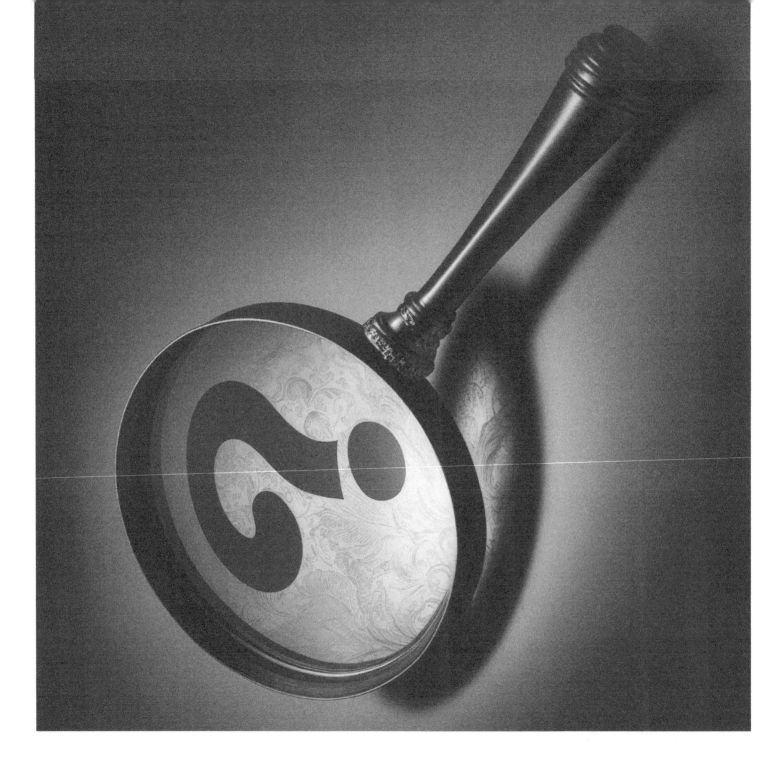

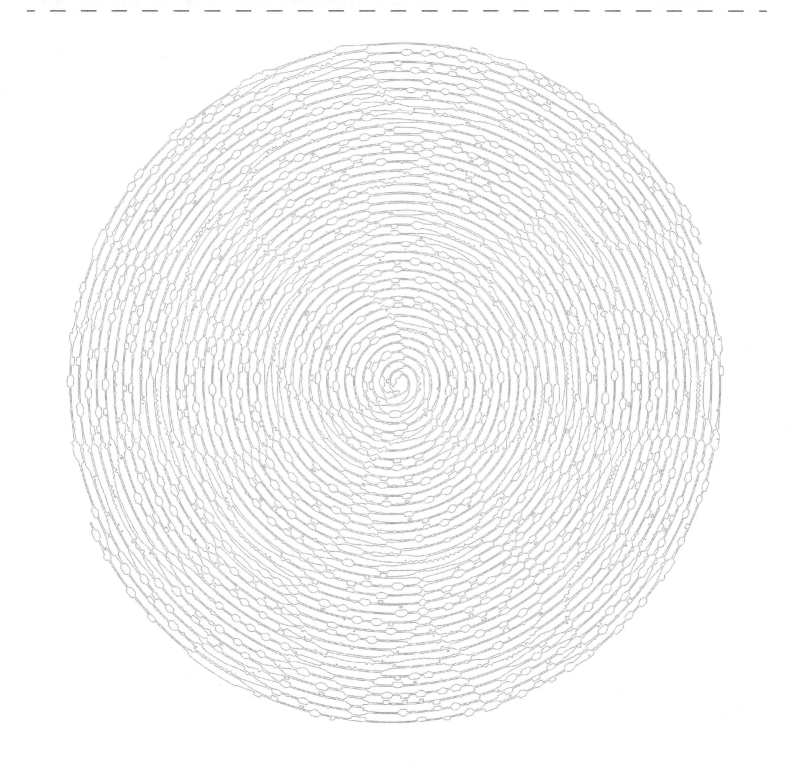

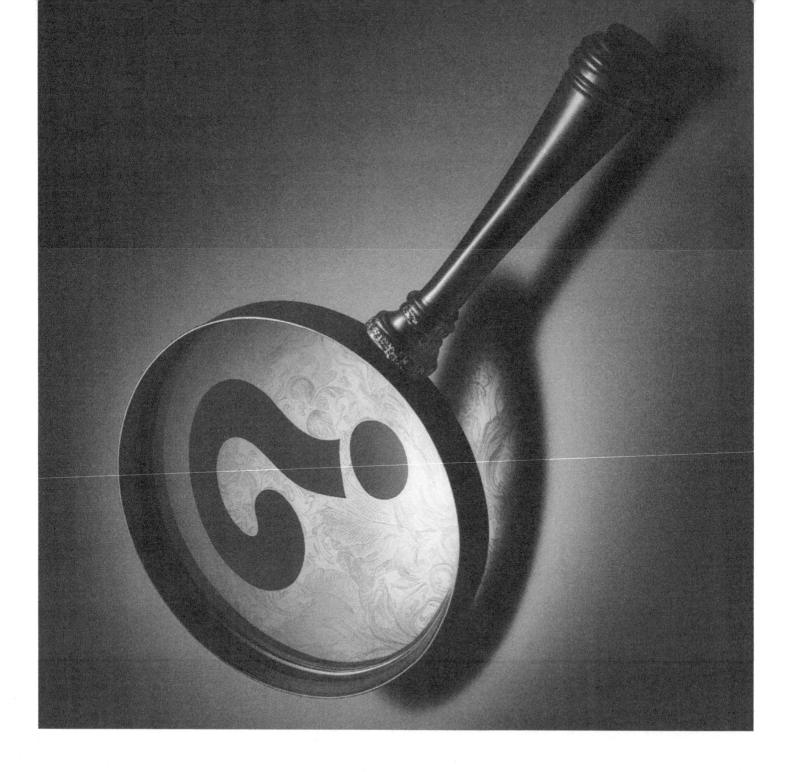

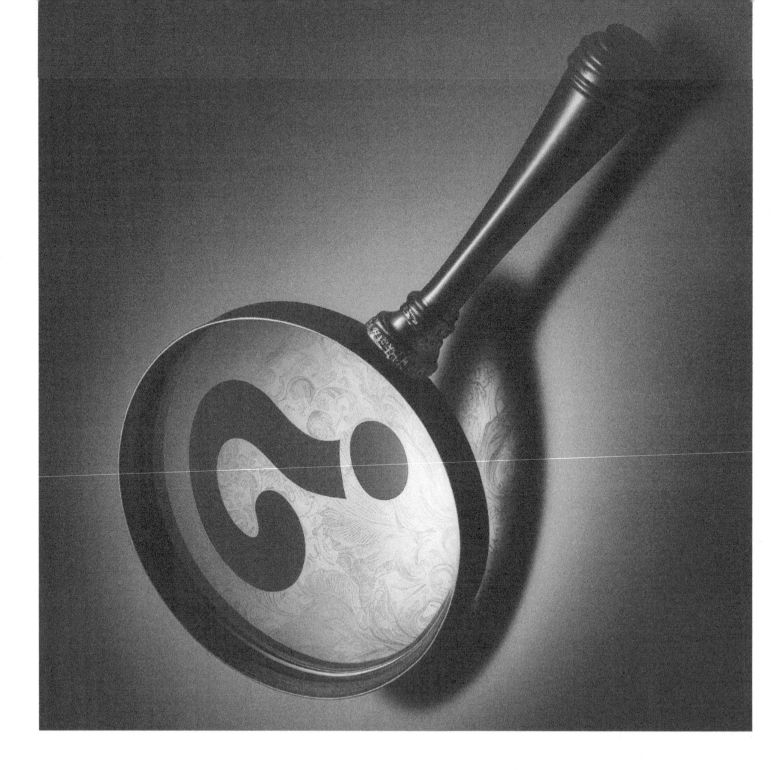

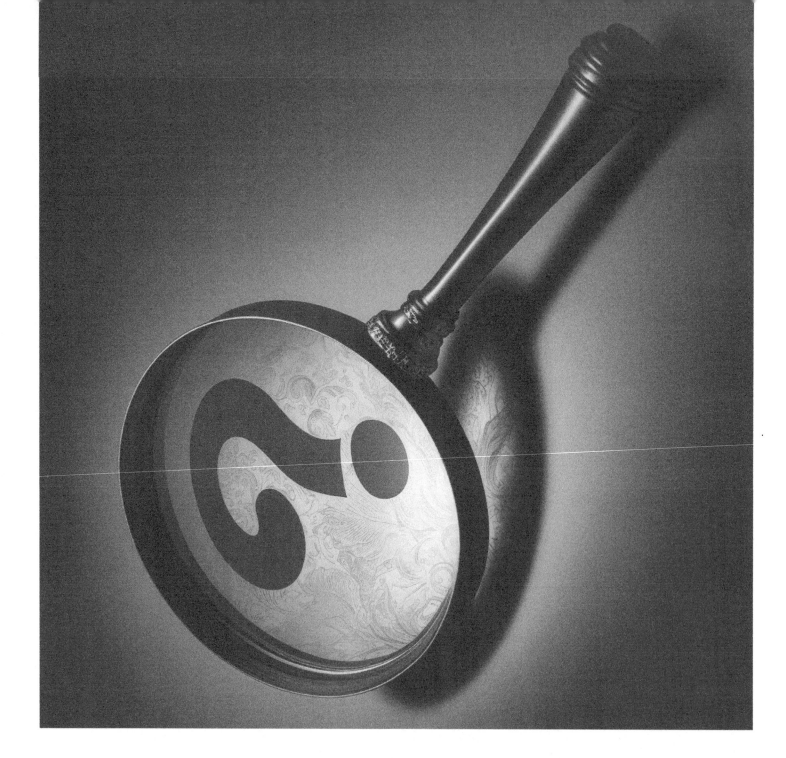

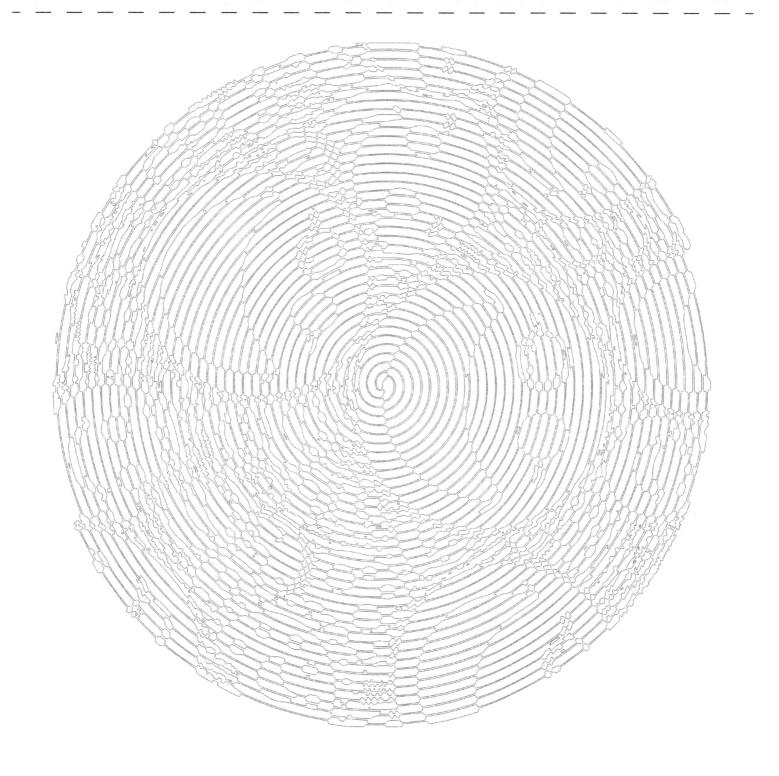

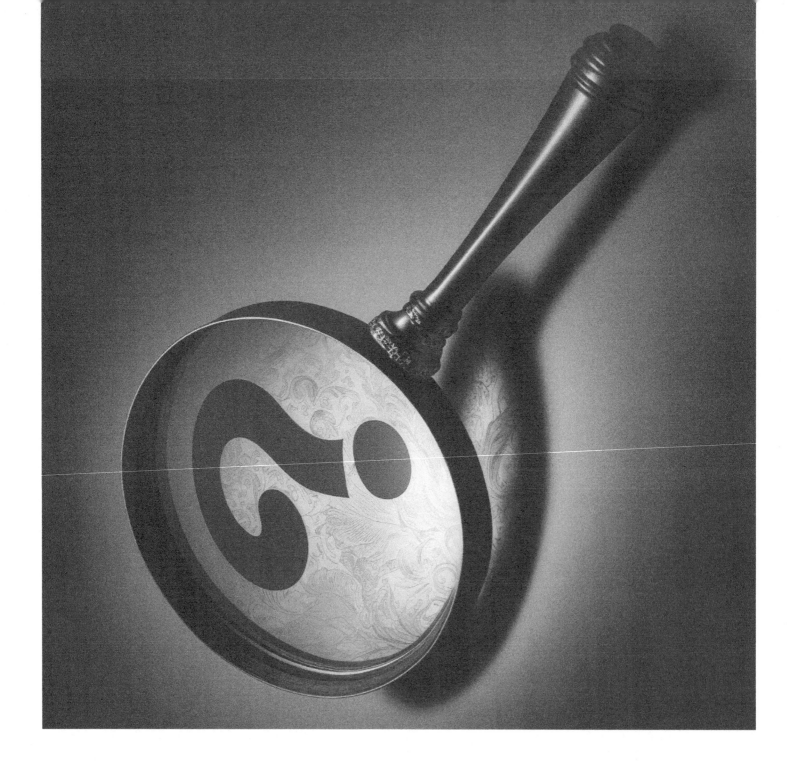

DID YOU ENJOY THIS ACTIVITY?

BUY VOLUME 1 OF THE I DON'T KNOW WHAT I'M COLORING! BOOK

LEAVE A REVIEW AND SUGGEST UNIVERSES TO EXPLORE!

I'LL MAKE A NEW BOOK AND YOU WON'T KNOW WHAT YOU'RE COLORING THEN, EITHER!

Made in the USA
Coppell, TX
28 April 2023

16187191R00031